Only From the Mind of a Mogul

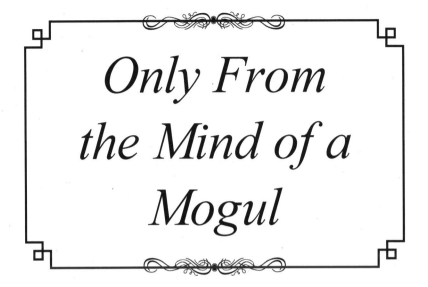

Only From the Mind of a Mogul

Nadine Judith Lynch

iUniverse

ONLY FROM THE MIND OF A MOGUL

iUniverse books may be ordered through booksellers or by contacting:

iUniverse
1663 Liberty Drive
Bloomington, IN 47403
www.iuniverse.com
1-800-Authors (1-800-288-4677)

Because of the dynamic nature of the Internet, any web addresses or links contained in this book may have changed since publication and may no longer be valid. The views expressed in this work are solely those of the author and do not necessarily reflect the views of the publisher, and the publisher hereby disclaims any responsibility for them.

Any people depicted in stock imagery provided by Thinkstock are models, and such images are being used for illustrative purposes only. Certain stock imagery © Thinkstock.

ISBN: 978-1-4917-2357-9 (Softcover)
ISBN: 978-1-4917-6688-0 (Audio)
ISBN: 978-1-4917-2358-6 (eBook)

Print information available on the last page.

iUniverse rev. date: 12/07/2015

Table of Contents

One way or another, this book will change your life.

Rumpled Foreskin

Lick my scrotum

I don't know them

I'm crème de la crème.

Bust a nut in my butt

I feel your bane in my gut,

come in my bum, cum in bum.

That's that hooker talk,

whoreism, hold your criticism,

street walker,

she got ticks in her draws,

let me hear all my female dogs bark

her pussy's so wet you gotta eat it with a spork

it cost more to fuck in the park before dark

everything is expensive in New York.

Welcome to the concrete jungle

what's that smell? It's ass cracks and sweaty balls in the concrete rumble

we bang cocks by the single

or by the bundle

me and my bitches grumble

rumpled foreskins packing our mouth making us mumble

it keeps us humble

like Bryant Gumble

we love to watch him fumble

like Urkel

giving his bitch a purple nurple

he dry hump her like a turtle

small niggas with big dicks stumble

their bitches' pussies stay crushed and crumpled

the size of their bulge make their I.Q. tumble

I ain't lookin for trouble

I'll triple what you double

quadruple

If you can spell that I'll suck you.

Me and your wifey tussle

two big cunts scuffle

her firm ass is supple

our celebrity titties cuddle

we fuck gay all day like Russell

that nigga love the bustle

drop a dime on his hustle

I spread eagle she suckle

watch her forehead bounce on my pelvic muscle

finger fuck me to the knuckle

making this bitch buckle,

I moan

she groan

I hit her up for a loan

give a she dog a bone

invite her to your home,

lay her down slow

lick her from head to toe

strap on the dildo

enter the dragon hustle and flow

say it's so Joe

fuck me Mandingo.

My Pussy's a Celebrity

Princess Pussy

certainly you realize what a cheesy dick does to me,

for sure

nymphos always want more

give me fifty you can score.

Princess Pussy with the Twisted Hook,

I joined the game enraged

to become a page

in Nas' rhyme book,

the man is a sage

he made me look,

internal gauge

stuck on Black rage

my verbiage got humatons shook.

Princess Big Rhed Pussy with the Twisted Hook,

pubes as long as spaghetti

shave that shit already.

I smell incense, frankincense and mur

Big Rhed, my pussy wears fur

it makes her purr

yes sir

I concur.

Big Rhed Pussy

pussy smoking a loosy

don't get mad at me

my pussy shot 50.

formerly known as Pussy Galore

I'm a whore

pussy juice is the lure.

I made my pussy a celebrity over night

always bet on black in a pussy fight

but I'm gonna bet on Rhed tonight

I am Big Rhed Pussy, come toward the light.

Respect my Girth

You come in gunnin'

bum rushin'

mean muggin'

like a female dog cummin'

you snuck in

duckin'

deep throatin'

queer crushin'

bum niggas bum rushin'

get you when you goin'

hit you when you runnin'

put it in your back cousin.

When you comin' down I'm gettin' higher

when you slidin' in I'm pullin' out, puttin' out fire

when you still cummin'

I'm goin'

I' gone,

when you still in her hole

I'm fuckin' in another home,

I stay creepin' in a zone

me and my dick roam alone.

I grip my bona

I wanna put my dick in ya.

Your modda is a mudder

ridin' dicks in the gutter

for a buck a hour,

she swalla a fella for whatever

your mother's clever.

Big Rhed Pussy

The man in the grey flannel suit

to boot

the point is moot

grab the loot,

I'm on the lam man, uncle Sam want you.

Ah choo

suck a rich Jew

commin' to finish you in the I.C.U,

tell the truth

I'm astute

in my blue zoot suite,

I'm so rude

I elude food

I'm in a bad mood

but I'm always smooth

thirsty niggas drool,

my pussy's huge,

she's Afrocentric like Erika Badu.

Over night success

Big Rhed Pussy in a blue dress

my D-cup breasts are decongestants.

Big Rhed bush

from the nation of Kush,

if you ain't one of us

you're just a big fat idiot like Rush.

Quid Pro Quo

Fe fi fo fum

quid pro quo chum

friends and foes cum

you suck me and I suck you some

watch my back son

while I scratch my snatch for fun.

Stop Looking at my Dick

Fuck your girl with my girth,

push her face in the dirt,

squirt dick juice on her silk shirt

spend all her self worth

respect my girth

respect what my moniker means on Earth.

I like to flirt

wipe my pussy with your dry cleaned shirt.

Cum spew

you're nobody 'till Big Rhed Fucks you,

balls swing

fuck a rich Jew for the Benjamins.

I ain't gone front

when I cum I grunt,

don't be shy

when I suck your dirty dick don't ever ask me why.

Slip it in slow slick

careful not to puncture your dick

while I pull out random dicks

from my New York bag of tricks.

Butt Fucking Bitches

Give a bitch a break, can a bitch not get butt fucked today?

Anyway

I don't go that way.

I love a bitch with balls, big, black and greasy

that don't break when they get licked to hard, you feel me.

I love a bitch with attitude,

that's that bitch in the red bottom shoes

I love a bitch with money

when the pussy runny

reminds me of me honey

funny

how she always fly and never fake

any chick this bitch want, this bitch take.

Vaginas in my Vision

can't beat em cheat 'em

can't screw em fuck 'em

can't love em leave 'em

can't change em kill 'em

we don't need 'em

we don't even believe 'em

we bleed 'em

we bag 'em and burn 'em

they don't shine, so we don't even see 'em

we pop our collars every time we defeat 'em.

Fake it till you make it, pretend

we're on to them

you're one of them.

I always use a condom

can't stand the smell of cum,

I got vaginas in my vision,

say hello to my big pum pum.

Tricks and Chicks and Dicks

I often wax poetic,

I don't dig dudes, but I enjoy a good dick,

fake or real, I don't give a shit.

Simon says I'm a lez,

I'm idolized by pedestrians,

my reality show breaks commandments,

I'm having a Laissez-Faire affair

with your mother's derriere.

Your bitch need her fix,

I be slipping your chick a mick

make her buck, make her kick,

she banned from sucking my pussy lips

after sucking on doggie dick like a tick,

gang banged by chicks with dicks

now her thick neck got a crick

would you like a phenzick?

Check if she sick,

make sure

before you take your dick out and raw fuck that fucking whore.

She mad insecure

she abject poor,

she used to be pure,

'till she let Al Gore bore her back door.

Ignore the mental image of guts and gore I explore

my pussy calls me Pussy Galore

after you get some, the bitch implore

please bitch, may I have some more?

Butt fucking is a chore

makes my asshole sore

I'd rather lay prostrate on your wife's kitchen floor.

For sheezy

my anus stay greasy

it ain't easy keeping my pussy cheesy,

for sure

it ain't easy being a ho no mo.

Respect my pussy,

respect the smell of dick on me

you smell me?

Get a whiff of my pussy

She's addictive like high technology.

Hey whatever

your mother's still clever

my pussy will live forever and ever.

Don't Hate me Because I'm Nasty

I take my pussy with me everywhere I go yo

never leave this bitch alone no,

when I chase the paper

I take her

when I need to cum for a nigga, I fake her.

This virgin bitch is my protege

word on the street, she gay.

Big Rhed Pussy with the Twisted Hook,

my pussy's booked.

My name is long y'all,

it takes up the whole wall

I'm dripping cum on the world from the pedestal.

Confusious say, my Big Rhed Pussy is nutritious and delicious,

My pussy is witty, charming and delightful,

yes she is, she's brilliant and beautiful,

too bad for you, what a pity

my pussy make lipstick look pretty.

You're an Animal

If she says she wonders,

if she says she needs,

If she says she like me,

give it to her Nadine.

It's your destiny to see me on TV

getting busy on top of Oprah Winfrey

getting head in the city like Mayor Diddy.

Every time she smiles she gives me a chubby,

of course I be cheating with her on my hubby

'cause I'm a phoney bitch nigga can't you see through me?

My Oozy Cry

I wear my holster at night

I wear my holster at night

so I can

so I can

carry my oozy by my side.

I wear my holster at night

I wear my holster at night

so I can

so I can

carry my oozy by my side.

Ooozy

ooozy

ooozy

ooozy.

My oozy cry

my oozy, cry

hear my oozy cry

hear my oozy, cry.

Ooozy

ooozy

ooozy

ooozy.

My oozy cry

my oozy, cry

hear my oozy cry

hear my oozy, cry.

Big Pun Intended

Big Pun, the Puerto Rican punisha

where you think you going miss his dick ain't done fucking ya,

crushing your girl in his basement

pushing her face in the cement,

half a ton a man keeping your pussy well fed.

A.K.A the Puerto Rican punishment

Puerto Rican know as the 11th commandment

bury your face in his excrement

mix your blood with the cement,

straight girls get bent,

gay girls get exactly what's coming to them,

lament,

repent,

where Big Pun crush Big Pun dent,

the Puerto Rican punishing

weapon of mass crushing,

don't be afraid of the penis miss,

I simply want you to feel this sis.

The paper and the pencils,

testicles bounce off my knuckles.

Word to my fist,

my rhymes is the shit,

I am that bitch,

what wrote this.

Big Rhed,

the shit from the toes to the head.

What!

Black Rage

See that nigga over there trying to hide,

he got a gun, he got black rage and he's high.

My Jamaican gun chatting

blood soaked bullets killing

preparing you for your viewing,

I admit it was kinda sick

the way I left you in repose on your posturepedic.

Come and see this

we did this,

Sealy can't believe it,

the Pope wanna bless it,

his mattress is holey.

It's dying time,

tomahawk to the hairline,

damn I rhyme tight,

with your insides outside resting in pieces on your Serta tonight,

you weak,

and you made a meat

my clip complete,

bloody white sheets.

Riot, slaughter, massacre, kill,

do it over and over again.

It's Dildo Time

It's t-shirt time

it's dildo time,

take off your clothes and fuck me with a phat rhyme,

may I lick your pussy since it's Christmas time?

I have big breasts on my chest.

My vagina has a first name,

it's eat me bitch!

My vagina has a last name,

it's how swollen is my clit?

Rude Gal Anthem

A weh de bloodclate

a weh de rassclate

a weh de bumboclate, cho!

Me nah romp wid yo bloodclate, yo no!

Me wi lick yo wid me pussyclate, cho cho.

A weh de bloodclate

a weh de rassclate

a weh de bumboclate, cho!

Me nah romp wid yo bloodclate, yo no!

Me wi lick yo wid me pussyclate, cho cho.

Now I've got the blues

I'm feeling used

you left me man

you left me for another woman,

but I feel no woes

'cause there's something both of us know

this Jamaican gal nah fight ova no man.

A weh de bloodclate

a weh de rassclate

a weh de bumboclate, cho!

Me nah romp wid yo bloodclate, yo no!

Me wi lick you wid me pussyclate, cho cho.

A weh de bloodclate

a weh de rassclate

a weh de bumboclate, cho!

Me nah romp wid yo bloodclate, yo no!

Me wi lick yo wid me pussyclate, cho cho.

Dip it Drip it

Me ago

Dip it pan yo lip

dip ina me whip

dip dip dip dip dip

dip me hip.

Me ago

Dip it pan yo gun

dip it pan yo son

dip dip dip dip dip

till me cum.

Me ago

Dip it pan Ms. Fierce

pan Jigga man face

dip dip dip dip

how me taste?

Me ago

Dip it pan yo buddy (dick)

dip it in yo money

dip dip dip dip

dip me pussy.

Me ago

Drip it when I'm high

drip it and lie

excuse me while I drip it on dis guy.

Me ago

Drip it pan yo madda

yo madda is a mudda

do you be dat nigga dat swalla?

Me ago

Drip it for a price

Natasha Nice came twice

I came thrice

drip drip drip

pussy hole drip dry.

Me ago

Drip it pan yo balls

drip pussy chemicals

drip cum on the world from the pedestals.

Over my Big Rhed Rass

Who do dat

who say dat,

a who say dem wan bus one ina my back,

wan lick a bitch when a bitch nah look

Big Rhed pussy wid de twisted Hook

come a foreign and write poetry book

dis gal can chat, and cook, and juk

me leave other pussy holes shook.

Rastafari know

you no seen though

how Nadine flow

make big man dem gwan like dem neva did know,

me been here before

yo no see my name pan de door

yo no see how I and I handle my microphone?

yo no see how me make de crowd dem galang pan de floor?

cho man you no want no more

all a uno know uno can't handle no more.

Everybody adore me

even de one who call herself mine enemy

de gal can't rhyme, she can't write nor read

If Jigga tighten her rhymes for a fee

who else she ago hire to make her fuck like me?

Death!

Here comes death

Him come fi claim you

death, do you know weh yo ago do?

Run, go home and get yo gun

think fast, death come fi capture yo ass

react quick, we ago drag yo ass ina it

look ina me eye, death don't lie

don't ask why

death just want you to die.

Impending Danger, Scared of what Made ya

Feel de terror in de air man

yo aim neva straight man

yo just too scared man

yo belly full a fear man

yo betta run away man

yo tampon tear man

de man a spill him guts ina him madda underwear man

wave yo pinky in de air man

yo just so dear man

bust a nut, here I cum ina yo sweet derriere man.

Juk

Everybody pull up a chair and look

'cause only Big Rhed know how fi juk

by the book

with one hand and don't look.

Lyrics I said

like lead

through yo head

pan yo bed

dead!

A who say dem want test Big Rhed?

In the Heart of the land

Have sex with your nipple

don't be simple

Bad Boyish smile with the one sided dimple

making ya dance, making the heartland jiggle

white people wiggle for sheezle

Rob Van Winkle, Kris Kringle, Vanilla Ice-cycle

Kip Kinkle, popping off hot nickel

when it go in yo back, it feel like a tickle

Make ya run when ya cripple

all the apple pies who live in the middle

feel the snow sizzle

sign o the times, bloody tinkle

pop, pop, pop, goes the armed American weasel

put a picture of the bloodbath on a easel

so all the world can see ya,

as your bloody trigger finger tremble,

everybody hate ya

they all want a piece a ya

they wanna beat ya

even ya teacher

the dead one beneath ya.

Living, the Bane of my Existing

Luke Woodham

woulda, coulda shoot em

had his parents for breakfast after he shoot em

went to school and schooled em

hunted his neighbors' children

he was friends with some of em

who got your back, here comes Woodham

he cocked the Gat, extra clips in his backpack

watch the bullets go through them

as Woodham do them

turned the insane pain into fame, now who the man, screw them

to quote woodham loosely

"now prison waiting for me

imprisoned to repay society

wondering daily

why everybody hate me

why everybody got it in for me

why everybody wanna kill me

who gone live for me

as I live in infamy

documented in history

actually turned painfully into infamy

forgive me

remember me

I had to do them for you to notice me

at least now you see me

or what's left of me in your memory

so hold my shit for me

while I pump one in me".

TheLynchDynasty.com

I make sin music, music to sin by

committing sins while you blast me on your wi-fi.

You gone want another piece of me,

hurting niggas like a gansta with a cavity

my rhyme style fuck up your reality,

hallucinate

about the pussies I ate

see a bitch fuck a bitch I'm sucking on her mammaries,

remember me? I'm reminding your memory

rewinding you memory

that bitch got it in for me

The Lynch Dynasty,

Pay the fee

buy my CD,

plus tax

Uncle Sam want his green back.

I'm a make Rap fun again

hold my dick! I'll load my gun again

lick my clit! I'm about to cum again

hold that bitch! this bitch wanna fuck again.

Focus in, focus out

focus in on my gun spout,

focus in on my ass bouncing off your chin

here I cum again.

Big Rhed

I write a verse everyday,

I slay it with rhymes, and rhythms, and Hip Hop ways,

I put a little butter

add a bit a sugar

and a whole lot of me make it better.

I like to pontificate

I like to penetrate

I like to levitate,

when I'm on the stage.

I drive a big car

'cause I'm a big star

I wanna go far

start a Rap war,

I like big things,

I got big tits,

I be a big bitch,

sucking on big dicks.

Do you be that Hermaphrodite-American?

Do you be that nigga that swalla?

do you remember the member that made you holla?

the first woman to squirt sperm on your blue collar?

do you be that hermaphrodite though,

wanna spread this bitch wide and lay your pussy dick low?

Me and my herma in the shower

busting a nut in my butt, I'm gonna live forever

Fucking feels as good as killing without shame

like a dark skinned nigga in the rain

seeking fame

in the game.

Here I cum again bend

I fuck cocks for ends,

I fuck bitches for free

I'm on a fucking spree

I'm fucking in the Matrix randomly.

Biggie

Dead niggas still bleed

even the dead smoke weed

like animals, we feed

we're the freed

we no longer care nor need,

Biggie crushed the Earth

with his girth

where Biggie walked, Biggie moved dirt.

16 Bars

1) These sixteen bars

2) left sixteen scars

3) on sixteen Rap stars

4) behind prison bars,

5) sixteen big niggas

6) butt fucked sixteen little wiggas,

7) my dick is as big as that nigga name Jigga.

8) Ivory soap float

9) fresh meat toss salads, don't rock the boat

10) D-block know, don't drop the soap.

11) Stop playing with my dick I use it to turn tricks,

12) spittin' is for kids,

13) before I start my show

14) I give out fellatio to every nigga I know,

15) form a line before I take the mic and shine,

16) Big Rhed, still the shit, from the toes to the head and the motherfucking bed.

My Mind is a Hell of a Find

Queen B bumble

I butt fucked her silly like Barney Rubble

crushed her down to his level

my cum is water soluble

don't be gullible,

I don't love ya

I just love to fuck ya,

make ya wobble

make this lazy eyed bitch see double

I'm as subtle

as a puddle

I'm easily corruptible,

I take bribes, I take lives,

like cops in a drunk huddle,

wilding in central park

after dark,

mugging a constable,

you can't CSI me,

my crimes are undetectable

y'all don't know me man, I'm unidentifiable

I make the Bible belt uncomfortable

the pain is unbearable

my shaved pussy got red stubble

I told ya, I'm as subtle as a poodle pissing in a puddle

I am the one, you're expendable,

you fuck fast

then haul ass

like Combustible Huxtable,

his dick got him in pussy trouble,

I am Big Rhed pussy, come toward the light, it's inevitable.

Cum on me

Give me fifty you can score

I'm a fucking whore

fucks galore

Elexis Monroe, can I have some more

in my back door?

Every day we trib in my crib,

she twist this bitch into the crush position at nights

like Sinn Sage in a fucking fuck fight,

me and Sinn Sage

locked in a sex cage

engaged in a sex rave,

pussy to pussy we grind in the tribulation times

committing sex crimes with my sex rhymes.

I like to get my pussy licked and sticked

by chicks with dicks

I'm sick

I'm fixed

you're congested, I'm Vick's,

I love it when a big pussy bitch cum on me,

the Matrix has you by the nuts, and the clits, and the wits

rub tits.

No more pussy for me Mom, I just ate,

I don't discriminate

but wait.

Remember dial up,

you think like DSL

I excel,

I'm with it like bandwidth.

I accelerate when I'm late

procrastinate to masturbate

wait.

Here comes the cum,

y'all contemplate

fetch a plate

a cup,

as I bisexually erupt.

By the way

my foreplay takes all day.

I gave my pussy hole a nick name

I'm vain.

For real,

don't fuck with my money honey,

it's my Achilles heel

only my diversified portfolio truly understands how I feel.

The Most Interesting Pussy in the World

I wanna talk about my pussy,

ever felt desire?

My pussy's on fire,

pussies make me wet

don't make me cum yet.

I want you to look at my pussy

lick my pussy, lick my pussy

a dingo ate my baby

a dingo ate my baby.

I wanna talk about my dick

let's talk about chicks with dicks

chicks with dicks and clits and tits.

I'm being black mailed

by a she-male,

she's a pretty white bitch with a big pussy dick.

The word is mum,

she never front,

but she tells the press that when I cum,

I grunt.

Oh girl swallow my sperm

and I'll pay to get you a perm

reward the bitch who give the best head

lesbian orgies on all my beds.

You know you owe me, every time you see me

every time you see me you owe me

bitch you betta bend ova

after J Hova

I still wanna fuck ya.

Don't act like you meek

or descended from the weak

motherfucker eat the pussy, destroy what you seek.

Nigga ride me hard,

treat me like a female dog,

slap my ass with your hairy balls.

Okey dokey,

here come another bitch who wanna choke me,

me and my bitches

stay tight like stitches,

we salivate

while we masturbate,

damn, my pussy got a headache,

aspirin deficiency,

chicks with dicks got it in for me

they wanna put it in me,

they wanna suck me and fuck me informally and frequently.

Your wifey slipped me a micky,

then bust a nut on my temple

the whole fuck smelled like what it resemble,

two pussies in a struggle

doing the boogle

after the fuck we smoke a loosy and snuggle.

Me and my mammaries

we mack on your salaries

creep up on your families

free them from their tragedies

abscond with your memories...

A.K.A The Pill

What's up everybody this is The Pill

I came to bring you the news from the hill

Congress say they gone pass a bill

they say my behavior is ill

cause I got x-rated skills.

I can't sit still

I just can't chill

I'm still on the pill

I wanna suck the wife of Mayor Bill.

You used to hit me on the hip, now hit me on the cell,

hit me on the motherfucking world wide web.

My pussy been around the corner, around the block, around the bend,

my pussy's very popular, she got a whole lot of friends.

I fly even when I ain't high,

you look familiar,

your dick looks like that guy.

I Got it All

I've got the i-phone, the i-pad and the i-pod

I've got the keys to my Beamer,

I've got the Mercedes Benz,

the BMW

the Rolls, the Maybach, and the Hum limo too.

What you see is not what you get,

it's what I call my special effect,

the Pill won't divulge everything yet.

I'm just a poetess with a cynical outlook,

a writer with a propensity for falsehood,

I specialize in fiction

contradiction

misrepresentation

inveracity,

mental dexterity,

these things are all me, baby.

I always lie,

I never cry,

sincerity is not my style,

never trust me or I'll rob you blind

if you leave me with your man I'll let him hit it from behind.

Dialectic Debris

Now let's talk about things that's hard to swallow

things that knock your world down and leave you to wallow,

things that make you cry,

things that make you think,

I know is hard to talk about these things.

And even though you write a little everyday

you try to make your way

you try to get through the day

but it's a struggle everyday by day,

'cause everything change,

nothing ever stays the same.

And if the sun don't rise tomorrow,

what cha gone do,

ain't no twenty four hours to borrow

you know you can't save some for tomorrow,

so you gotta live life,

you cant waste no more time.

Oh my When Kanye West Smiles

(A Nadine Judith Lynch and Christina Nelson Collaboration)

He's not quite what he seems,

because when he's smiling

he's not even trying

yet his entire being beams.

It's rare and it's real

it's revered when revealed,

and in those moments

it's your heart that he steals

then you feel exactly how he feels.

It is captivating, awe-inspiring and life-altering,

it's the anti-weapon, the tool of mass construction,

it builds nations and heals fractured relations.

Perhaps George W. Bush doesn't care about black people as Kanye said,

however, when Kanye smiles even Bush's cheeks turn red.

Kanye's smile compensates

because North's fans rarely see a smile on her adorable yet serious face.

Imagine the allure of King Kanye's smile on mount Rushmore

for all to adore,

and on the American flag

and on the U.S. Dollars in your Givenchy bag.

It brings people together and makes life better

it's a national treasure

that we will selfie forever.

In the meanwhile, patiently I beguile

as I tenaciously await Kanye's next smile.

It's a thing of beauty

even more illuminating than Kardashian booty.

Kanye loves to compose a $mize

whilst he cooly negotiates between Kimye's thighs.

And when he asked Kim to marry him

he didn't need that million dollar ring

all he needed was that exquisite thing

his sweet, disarming, charming grin

just flash that sincere $mile for the win

that priceless bling, bling, bling.

And wow can the King sing,

Yeezus slays us with his haunting melodies

then pumps us with the remedies

resurrecting us with his smile all the while.

To Swiftly tackle the Taylor debacle,

what if he had tossed her a $mirk

when he hi-jacked the VMA mic on that historic MTV night?

Even President Obama said that he behaved like a jerk,

but was Kanye right about what he had said?

What if he had simply slipped her a Kanye smile instead?

Mollified Molly with it like a pillow on a bed,

hypnotized her

Kanyed her

got in her head.

Ode to Dick

I like the dicks with the hood hat

that look like they wearing a NY cap

I like the dicks that fuck black

like a bitch in the hood who fuck back

I like the dicks that are well fed

that are thick like Jamaican hard dough bread (give head).

I like the dicks that are mean

my pussy is a dick fiend

I like a dick with a facial scar

that looks like it's going to war

even if my pussy's far

she'll leave the door ajar

my pussy's fat like Roseanne Barr

and fits more mexican dicks than a clown car

I like the dicks that fuck raw

that can't be see on your man's gaydar.

Dick is good

dick is best in the hood

from the shaft to the head

fuck me on your bitch's bed

cum on my head.

It was me getting fucked on the bathroom floor

by the dick next door.

I'm Big Rhed Pussy With the Twisted Hook

I love to juk

by dicks that ain't shook

my pussy reads books

she's an intellectual

like a dick that's effectual.

Never dull

got pull

wears wool

my pussy's full.

I got my good eye on my woman

I got my money in my right hand,

I'm gripping my dick

stepping in my blue kicks,

which big clit bitch

do I have to suck to produce this hit?

The Bronx

Biggie said "my borough is through"

Big Rhed contend, New York City got the prettiest titties.

We be getting jiggy with it

more jiggier than Will Smithy with it

the Boogie Down, yeah I be fucking with it

I reside in it

I rep it and I rhyme in boogie down time for it

I sweat in it

bleed in it

and cry in it

I spend quality time with it

as if I gave birth to it

I love it

protect it

and nurture it

it's got nature in it

just like Brooklyn got a tree growing in it

I smoke my weed in it

en el Bronx, the weed got less seeds in it

Every Time you See me you Owe me

I eat your share while you look at me

I sit in your chair while you look at me

I suck your chick while you look at me

I take over your world while you look at me

God damn, wow just look at me

I know y'all like to look at me

just shut up and look at me

TV was made so you could get to look at me

I was meticulously sculpted exquisitely for you to look at me

see the fee you'll have to pay just to look at me

he gets a stiffy every time he looks at me

she gets a wetty every time she looks at me

Youtube me to look at me

Nadine likes to look at me

everybody Googles me to look at me

every time you see me you owe me

look at me!

Pussy on Layaway

Your wifey rang me on the tele

told me she was ready

want to come and put my pussy on her belly.

Though she couldn't pay

she needed me to come anyway

so I said OK

let me ask my pussy what she has to say.

Even with an I.O.U

you can own a little piece of my pussy too.

Never underestimate what money can do

my money long too

longer than the joint in your pants too

I don't need to use you

I already own you

I already fucked you

I experienced you

'cause my girlfriend told me you fuck good too,

'cause you got money

I let you into my pussy.

I'm Just That Gal

Whole heap a big Shirley a cum pan me early, everyday

me know how them like it gal and me know what to do and say

them think say me gay

by the things weh me do and say

me say me ago gay for today

and when gay gal pay my way.

Me come ya so fi dig ina yo Ital pot

me come fi lick yo pussy 'till me jaw bone lock

me come ya so fi let yo man blow out me back

me come ya so fi swallow jizzum when him ejac

me come ya so fi test how yo girl pussy rock

sex contract,

I and I like man hairy with a big ugly cock

squirt your sperm pan me new brand frock

me pussy unlock

me have a big rack

yo big ugly buddy betta hit the g-spot

me ready for the big buddy anal attack

ina the back of the Benz

with the doors unlock

Lard me slack,

weh the gal them weh gay

and fuck man anyway?

Epiphany (The Cocky Dick)

Epiphany

pull yo buddy out and shub it ina me

uh

big buddy nigga bust off up ina me

him a cum ina me

uh

long tongue nigga suck out ina me

uh

nigga buddy betta back door me

uh.

Another epiphany

take yo buddy outta me

and neva put it ina me

uh

neva let nigga bust off up ina me

him nah cum ina me

uh

neva let nigga suck out ina me

uh

neva let nigga back door me

uh.

Making my Case

Get out of my face

before I tear a space

between you and my mace.

Printed in the United States
By Bookmasters